OJIBWE

—

Sierra Adare

Gareth Stevens Publishing

A WORLD ALMANAC EDUCATION GROUP COMPANY

Please visit our web site at: www.garethstevens.com
For a free color catalog describing Gareth Stevens Publishing's list of high-quality books
and multimedia programs, call 1-800-542-2595 (USA) or 1-800-387-3178 (Canada).
Gareth Stevens Publishing's fax: (414) 332-3567.

Library of Congress Cataloging-in-Publication Data

Adare, Sierra.
    Ojibwe / by Sierra Adare.
        p. cm. — (Native American peoples)
    Summary: A discussion of the history, culture, and contemporary life of the
Ojibwe Indians.
    Includes bibliographical references and index.
    ISBN 0-8368-3667-7 (lib. bdg.)
    1. Ojibwa Indians—History—Juvenile literature. 2. Ojibwa Indians—Social
life and customs—Juvenile literature. [1. Ojibwa Indians.] I. Title. II. Series.
E99.C6A33   2003
979.004'973—dc21   2002191112

First published in 2003 by
Gareth Stevens Publishing
A World Almanac Education Group Company
330 West Olive Street, Suite 100
Milwaukee, WI 53212 USA

Produced by Discovery Books
Editor: Valerie J. Weber
Series designer: Sabine Beaupré
Designer and page production: Ian Winton
Photo researcher: Rachel Tisdale
Native American consultant: D. L. Birchfield, J.D., Associate Professor of Native American
    Studies at the University of Lethbridge, Alberta
Maps and diagrams: Stefan Chabluk
Gareth Stevens editorial direction: Mark Sachner
Gareth Stevens art direction: Tammy Gruenewald
Gareth Stevens production: Jessica L. Yanke

Photo credits: Sierra Adare: p. 13 (bottom); Allsport: p. 25 (bottom); Corbis: cover, pp. 4, 7, 9,
13 (top), 15, 16, 20, 21, 26, 27 (top); Mille Lacs Band (Minnesota): pp. 5, 10, 11, 17,
18, 19, 23, 24, 25 (top), 27 (bottom); Peter Newark's American Pictures: p. 8; North Wind
Picture Archives: p. 6; Sun Valley/Native Stock Photography: pp. 12, 14.

Printed in the United States of America

1 2 3 4 5 6 7 8 9 07 06 05 04 03

Cover: A young Ojibwe man wearing traditional dress at a powwow at Lake Leech, Minnesota.

Contents

Words that appear in the glossary are printed in
boldface type the first time they appear in the text.

Origins

A young Ojibwe man wearing traditional dress at a powwow at Lake Leech in Minnesota.

Land of the Ojibwes

One of the most numerous of the Native populations in North America, the Ojibwes (oh-JIB-ways) are scattered across the United States and Canada. The Ojibwe, Potawatomi, and Ottawa peoples were originally one people. Their traditional territory stretched from the northern Great Plains near present-day Lake Winnepeg in Manitoba, Canada, to the southeastern shores of the Great Lakes in today's United States and from central Saskatchewan to southern Ontario in today's Canada.

No one knows exactly how the Ojibwes and other Native Americans came to North America. Like most Native peoples, though, Ojibwes tell a traditional story to explain their origins: long ago, only water covered the earth. Creator's helper, called Naanabozho, and his friends were floating on a raft. Naanabozho asked his friends to dive under the water and get some earth. Many tried and failed. Then Muskrat dived down and came back with sand in his paws. Naanabozho blew on the sand, spreading it over the water to create dry land. Muskrat kept diving for sand, and

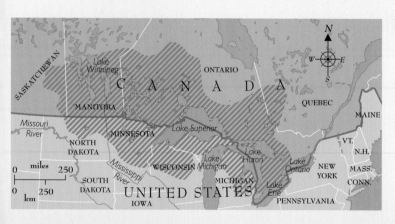

The shaded area on this map shows the traditional lands of the Ojibwe people.

Speaking Ojibwe

Ojibwe	Pronunciation	English
aneen	ah neen	hello
e yah'	ee yah	yes
gaween	gah ween	no
abinojeyag	a bin new je yag	children
mii gwetch	me gwetch	thank you
ogema	o ge ma	leader of an Anishinaabe band or chief
aki	ah key	land
nibi	ne be	water

Naanabozho kept blowing on it until the land was large enough to support people.

Several scientific theories explore the possible origins of the Ojibwes and other Native Americans. The most popular theory is that thousands of years ago, people crossed a land mass between Asia and North America in the region now called the Bering Strait. Other scientists think that Native Americans might have come to the Americas by sea. They would have then migrated on foot across South, Central, and North America.

Many Names, One People

The Ojibwes, also known as the Chippewas, call themselves Anishinaabe (ah-nish-na-bay) or its plural, Anishinaabeg, which means "the people." They prefer to be called Anishinaabe rather than Ojibwe or Chippewa.

Examples of traditional Ojibwe moccasins. Some non-Native historians have suggested that the words *Chippewa* and *Ojibwe* (also spelled *Ojibway* and *Ojibwa*) are translations for the term "puckered up" that describes the style of the Ojibwe moccasin.

History

Long before contact with Europeans, an Anishinaabe **elder prophesied** "white spirits would come in numbers like sand on the lake shore, and would sweep the red race from the hunting grounds which the Great Spirit had given them."

Ojibwe (Anishinaabe) historian William Warren

Early Contact with Europeans

Europeans came to North America from the late fifteenth century onward, hoping for new land, ways to acquire wealth, or religious freedom. The French began exploring the North American continent in the early 1600s looking for furs. Wanting to trade, they first came into contact with the Ojibwes (Anishinaabeg) in 1622. The traders and the Ojibwes soon built a strong **alliance** that benefited both peoples; the French got furs, while the Ojibwes received guns and other trade goods such as cast iron pots, iron axes, and blankets. Guns helped the Ojibwes defend their territory.

Woodcut of a French fur trader's camp. The Ojibwe were excellent hunters and trappers and through their trade with the French they became powerful and wealthy.

The Ojibwes even kept out the powerful Haudenosaunees, Native peoples being pushed from their land by invading Europeans (especially Dutch and British) settling on Haudenosaunee land along the East Coast. The Europeans pushed the Haudenosaunees (called Iroquois by the Eurpoeans) into the eastern side of the Ojibwes' territory in what is now Michigan.

Many of the wilderness areas of the lakes and woods of Minnesota and Wisconsin have hardly changed since the time when the Ojibwes and Europeans first met.

In 1679, French trader Daniel du Luth persuaded Ojibwe leaders to attend a council with the Dakota-speaking people of the Seven Bands of the Teton. Du Luth helped these two traditional enemies form an alliance. Peace brought stability to the region and allowed for more trading with the French. The Ojibwes gained more hunting grounds to the west in Dakota-held territory in today's northern Minnesota and Wisconsin, while the Dakotas received a steadier supply of trade goods from the French.

Woodcut of Ojibwe women in a birch-bark canoe gathering wild rice.

A People on the Move

As the French fur trade moved westward, so did the Ojibwes.
They spread out into the Great Lakes, the Great Plains, and
what is now Michigan and Wisconsin in the United States and
Ontario, Canada. Although this move resulted in a series of
disputes between the Ojibwes and their neighbors, the Ojibwe-
Dakota alliance lasted until 1736, when the Dakotas broke with
the Ojibwes and the French over trade and land issues, killing
twenty-one French allies. By 1750, the Ojibwes were occupying
the land held by the Dakotas.

As more whites illegally moved onto Natives' land, the
Ojibwes battled the Dakotas and other neighboring tribes
over rights to the remaining hunting land from the mid-1700s
to the mid-1800s. Fights such as the Battle of the Brulé in 1842
eventually resulted in Ojibwes permanently driving the Dakotas
west across the Mississippi River.

The British, French, and Americans Battle

The Ojibwes also joined the French in trying to push the British from Canada during the French and Indian War (1754-1763), but the British took control of Canada from the French in 1760. In the Proclamation of 1763, the British recognized the Ojibwes' right to their own territory. By 1800, however, the British had forced the Ojibwes to give up over 5,000,000 acres (over 2,000,000 hectares) in Canada.

In 1776, the British and the Americans went to war over who would control the colonies in America. The Americans, with the help of many **indigenous** nations, won the war and became the United States. The Treaty of Paris, signed at the end of the American Revolution (1783), established the boundaries between the United States and Canada, splitting the Ojibwes' territories between the two countries.

Although you have conquered the French, you have not conquered us. We are not your slaves. These lakes, these woods and mountains were left us by our **ancestors** . . . and we will part with them to none.

Ojibwe (Anishinaabe) leader Minweweh in response to the British takeover of Canada in 1760

Native peoples sided with either the British or the French in the French and Indian War (1754–1763). British success in this war meant the Ojibwes were soon forced to give up large areas of their territory.

Life was hard for the Ojibwes during the nineteenth century as they were forced to give up more and more land to the U.S. and Canadian governments. This family was photographed in its home on a reservation in 1900.

Governments Force Removal

Through **treaties**, both the Americans and the British in Canada forced the Ojibwes to give up land. The U.S. and Canadian governments also wanted the Ojibwes to take up Euro-American-style farming and live in what the British called "model villages."

The 1850 Robinson Superior Treaty

Ex-fur trader William Robinson **negotiated** a treaty between the Ojibwes (Anishinaabeg) living near Lake Superior and the Canadian government. In the treaty, the Ojibwes agreed to give the government some land. In return, the Canadians agreed that each Ojibwe band could select its own reservation site and each member of the bands would receive money for the land signed over to the government. The Canadians also promised that the Ojibwes would always be allowed to hunt and fish on those lands the Ojibwes gave to the government. Like many treaties, this one was quickly broken. Ojibwes were kept from hunting and fishing on the lands given to the government. As non-Natives moved onto the reservations, they took more land from the Ojibwes and the reservations shrank in size or disappeared.

These villages were designed to force the Ojibwes to **assimilate** — to live like Euro-Americans and give up their tribal customs. By 1900, treaties had forced Ojibwes to move onto reservations. However, neither government stopped whites from illegally settling on Ojibwe land.

Reservation Life

The Canadian and U.S. governments broke their treaties with the Ojibwes. They allowed whites to illegally settle on the reservations, cutting down the timber, mining minerals, and destroying the Ojibwes' rice fields and sugar maple trees. This made life hard for Ojibwes, who were used to living in an environment that provided plenty of food.

By the early 1900s, the Ojibwes were starving. Although part of both governments' plans included teaching Ojibwes European-American farming methods, what little reservation land that was left was often too poor to farm. Sometimes there was not even enough land to both live on and farm.

Conditions on the early reservations were harsh. Many people were forced to live in homes that were little more than shacks.

Boarding Schools

Canada and the United States passed laws forcing Ojibwes to send their children to boarding schools. Between the 1880s and 1940s, children as young as four were removed from their families. At school, children were punished for speaking their language. Boys spent summers working as laborers for white farmers or factory owners, while girls worked as maids. They worked long hours and received little or no money for their labor.

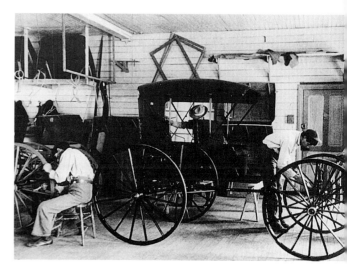

Boys working in the blacksmith shop of an Indian boarding school. In an attempt to destroy Native American culture, many Ojibwe children were forced to leave their homes and families and go to boarding schools set up by the U.S. and Canadian governments.

Many were not allowed to return home until they were eighteen. The Ojibwes, however, managed to hold onto their culture.

Relocation to the Cities

In the 1950s, the United States government moved families from reservations to large cities in what the government called the "Volunteer Relocation Program" so the government could claim more of the Ojibwes' land. The program was anything but voluntary. Many Ojibwes were actually forced to move to cities such as Minneapolis and St. Paul in Minnesota. By 1970, approximately half of the Ojibwes had been moved off reservations and into urban centers.

The American Indian Movement (AIM) arose out of the government's pressure on these "urban Indians" to fully assimilate into white culture. Three Ojibwes — Dennis Banks, Clyde Bellecourt, and George Mitchell — founded AIM in Minneapolis in 1968. AIM's goal was to help Ojibwe children

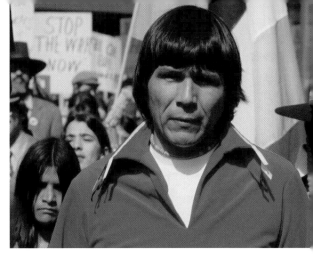

Dennis Banks, one of the founders of the American Indian Movement that demanded that the government review treaties made between the United States and Native Americans.

learn more about their own culture, language, and traditions.

The idea spread to other urban Natives interested in keeping their cultures alive. By 1971, AIM had become a national organization and included Natives on reservations and in rural areas. Their goals grew too. AIM wanted to protect the traditions of all indigenous peoples. One way AIM and its supporters accomplished this was to bring legal cases to court, trying to get the government to uphold indigenous treaty rights such as the tribes' right to hunt, fish, and gather wild rice on their traditional lands as guaranteed by treaties.

Adam Fortunate Eagle

In 1969, Ojibwe (Anishinaabe) Adam Fortunate Eagle was among AIM members from many indigenous nations attempting to bring worldwide attention to Native peoples' treaty rights. One treaty right allowed Natives to move to and live on land abandoned by the federal government. Alcatraz Island off the coast of California had been a prison that the government had abandoned. AIM wanted to use that land to build a Center for Native American Studies, an indigenous museum, and a school where Native children could learn the history, traditions, and language of their tribes. AIM members, including Fortunate Eagle, lived on Alcatraz Island for nineteen months before the government cut off their supply of food and water and forced them to leave. The government has never allowed the center, museum, and school to be built.

Traditional
Way of Life

A historic photograph of an Ojibwe woman at a sugar bush camp, cooking down the maple sap to make syrup and sugar.

A Seasonal Lifestyle

For centuries, individual Ojibwe (Anishinaabe) bands moved with the seasons. Over winter, they hunted and got furs ready for trading by scraping and **tanning** them. In spring, "sugar bush" camp reunited friends and families. Relatives gathered at the family's own section of maple forest. They tapped trees and collected sap in birch-bark containers, then boiled the sap down into syrup. Once this hardened, they put it in wooden troughs and used big wooden spoons to pound it into sugar. Each family processed 500 to 600 pounds (225 to 270 kilograms) of maple sugar annually.

Ojibwe craftspeople still make traditional birch-bark canoes as a way of keeping their culture alive. Here bark is being sewn over the canoe frame with spruce thread. Birch-bark canoes are surprisingly lightweight. A canoe intended to carry nine people can itself be carried by just one person!

In summer, villages north of Lakes Superior and Huron provided a base from which families went fishing. Women made basswood-twine nets that they fished with. After catching the fish, the women washed the nets in a sumac-leaf solution to destroy fish odor, making sure fish would not shy away from the nets next time. Men made deer-bone hooks for fishing with poles, and in winter, they used wooden, fish-shaped decoys to lure fish to holes cut in the ice. When the waters were clear of ice, they also spearfished at night, seeing by birch-bark torches placed at the front of their canoes.

While men fished, women grew pumpkins, sweet potatoes, corn, beans, and squash. In autumn, they harvested wild foods such as nuts, berries, and rice. This was also a time for gathering herbs the people used for medicines such as goldenseal and purple coneflower, which were used to treat colds. This seasonal life remained central to Ojibwes until into the twentieth century.

The Prophecy of the Sacred Megis Shells

Megis shells were used to barter for trade goods such as pottery, conch shells, copper, turquoise, and other precious stones with other Native peoples. The shells strung on **wampum belts** served as written records and treaties. In Ojibwe (Anishinaabe) oral history, Creator told the people to follow the megis shells west from their homeland along today's St. Lawrence River until they found a place where "food grows on water." The shells led the Ojibwes to the wild rice, growing in what is now Minnesota.

Home Life

Ojibwes lived in a dome-shaped house called a *wigwasigamig*. Bending wooden poles into a frame, they covered the frame with woven mats made from birch bark and cattails. A large wigwasigamig held several families. Europeans mispronounced the Ojibwes' word for their homes, calling them wigwams.

The Ojibwes made clothing from deerskins. Men wore a loincloth, leggings, and moccasins, while women made and wore sleeveless dresses over soft, nettle-fiber undershirts, leggings, and moccasins. The women stripped the nettle stalks and used the dried inner fibers of the plants to make clothes, somewhat like spinning wool into yarn that is then woven into cloth. In winter, people added buckskin robes. Porcupine quills decorated clothing. Trade blankets were later made into coats, pants eventually replaced leggings, and women made their dresses and leggings out of **broadcloth**. Seed beads in complex floral patterns became more common on clothing after the beads became a trade item in the mid-seventeenth century.

This Ojibwe couple, photographed in 1900, are standing in front of their wigwasigamig home. Whites had stolen so much of the Ojibwes' land, destroying their rice fields and sugar bush camps, that Ojibwe communities became among the poorest in North America during the 1900s.

A historic picture of an Ojibwe family. The young woman is wearing traditional dress, but the photographer who took the picture probably insisted she wore the feathers and a headband even though this is not traditional for the Ojibwes.

> As was customary in the Indian community, my grandparents also helped raise several of their grandchildren and sometimes provided a home for other extended family members. They taught their children about the northern seasons, hard work, generosity, the value of relatives, and they imparted stories and songs, all in the Ojibwe language.
>
> *Brenda Child, in* Boarding School Seasons, *1995*

Family Life

Ojibwes lived in family groups called **clans**. Clans were patrilineal, which means that the children belonged to their father's clan. People could not marry within their own clan. Several clans lived together in what is called a band. Friends and relatives who married into other bands often visited each other. Bands also came together for religious ceremonies, feasts, and social dances. These events gave young people opportunities to meet. Many bands make up the Ojibwe Nation.

Family values were strong among Ojibwes. Grandparents took part in raising children. White travelers often commented on Ojibwes' great affection for their children. "Even fathers are very kind to their sons," wrote one man. He added that children were quiet and polite. Children played with cornhusk dolls and ducks made out of cattails by relatives.

Government

Ojibwe bands acted independently of one other. Each elected its own leader, the *Ogimah*, and his advisers, called *Anikeh-Ogimauk*. Leaders were chosen by **consensus**, meaning the people all agreed on who the leaders would be. The people selected leaders who were considerate, wise, and willing to put the needs of the people first.

This photograph, taken sometime near the end of the nineteenth century, shows the Ojibwe Chief Skinaway (left, with arms folded). The man with the drum is Chief Wadena, who, in 1902, led a protest against the government's forced removal of the Ojibwes from the Mille Lacs Band Reservation to White Earth Reservation. Both men have been photographed wearing non-Ojibwe feathered headdresses.

When the U.S. and Canadian governments began treaty negotiations, Ojibwes found that whites expected to deal with a single tribal leader. They forced the Ojibwes to change their traditional government. Bands formed what became known as the Grand Council and elected a primary Ogimah. The Grand Council was responsible for declaring war, negotiating peace, and developing laws.

Sam Yankee, Ojibwe Leader

Sam Yankee's Ojibwe (Anishinaabe) name was Ayshpun, meaning "very high up." Born sometime around 1900, Ayshpun was a Midé, a religious leader in the Midewiwin, a group of healers. He also had the honor of being a drum carrier, the person chosen to care for the ceremonial drum.

The Mille Lacs Band of Ojibwe Indians in Minnesota elected him chair of the Reservation Business Committee, part of the Mille Lacs' government. Its members oversee tribal affairs. Ayshpun helped develop programs that resulted in building new homes for band members and a community center where children could learn Ojibwe traditions. He also taught the language, traditional songs, and drumming, and he shared the oral history of the people with youngsters. Ayshpun led his people during the 1960s and 1970s, a time of great change.

Beliefs

Many Ojibwes believe in the Creator, who is neither male nor female. The Creator shares power with others — the trees, plants, animals, water, other spirits, and people — that are often messengers for the Creator, bringing the Midewiwin (a religious society of healers) dreams and spirit guides.

Dreams are an important part of Ojibwe religious beliefs. Boys and girls are encouraged to seek **visions**. During vision **quests**, Ojibwes receive dreams. They may also receive special lessons from an animal who becomes their spirit guide, or they may be shown how to use a medicine plant in a new way. A spirit guide comes to a person when and how the spirit guide decides.

Ojibwe women, wearing Jingle dresses, perform dances at their powwow at the Leech Lake Reservation in Minnesota. The Jingle dress is sacred to the Ojibwes and originates from an old story about an elder who received a vision telling him to make a dress that jingled for his sick daughter.

Traditional Healers

Depending on local traditions, there are four or eight levels of membership in the Midewiwin. Members are called Midé. They advance by completing lessons in proper behavior and in identifying and using medicines. They also learn how to read Midewiwin records written on birch-bark scrolls. Those at the highest levels know how to use rare herbs.

"Ojibwe Tea"

The Midewiwin believe that living a patient, moderate, truthful, and respectful life, combined with using medicine plants given by the Creator, prolongs life. In the 1930s, a white nurse named Renee Caisse treated very sick patients with a blend of herbs the Midewiwin use. She called this blend "Ojibwe tea." The recovery rate was impressive. Scientific studies show "Ojibwe tea" reduces pain and increases the number of cells that fight diseases. The herbs in "Ojibwe tea" are some of the 637 herbs used by **indigenous** peoples that have been accepted for use by the United States government.

The society used to hold ceremonies in a special lodge that was not covered unless the weather was bad. This way non-members could view them. However, the Midé conducted ceremonies in a special language with special songs that only members understand.

Among Ojibwes, Native healers have traditionally been given the same respect as modern-day doctors because they can use herbs to treat sickness in people and bring them back to health. To become an Ojibwe healer takes a lifetime of education and practice.

Midewiwin healer Maymasushkowaush, known to whites as Axel Pasey, poses with his wife and daughter in this 1936 photo. Although he wears traditional clothing, the feathers and headbands are not traditional Ojibwe. Many whites believed all Indians wore feathers.

Today

Ojibwe Governments

Today, about 120,000 Ojibwes (Anishinaabeg) live in Michigan, Wisconsin, Minnesota, and North Dakota in the United States and about 40,000 in southern Ontario. Each Ojibwe reservation in Canada elects its own Ogimah and council. The reservations (called reserves in Canada) also send representatives to the Union of Ontario Indians (UOI). UOI works with the Canadian government, trying to insure that the indigenous peoples receive the health and educational programs to which they are entitled.

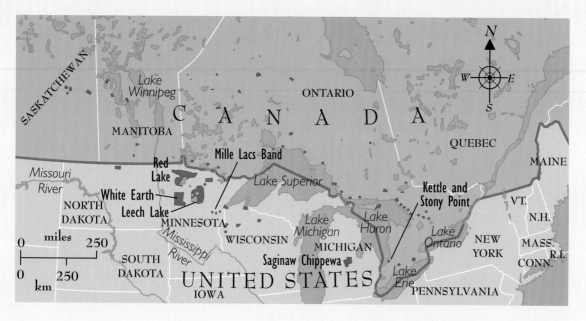

The red areas on this map mark where most of the Ojibwe reservations are today.

In the United States, individual Ojibwe bands elect tribal councils consisting of a board with a chairperson. The Mille Lacs Band in Minnesota, however, has a governmental system similar to that of the United States.

Treaty Rights

In the 1980s, Ojibwes began taking the U.S. and Canadian governments to court over broken treaties. The Ojibwes proved in court that they had the right, as stated in the 1837 and 1850 treaties, to hunt and fish on the lands turned over to the U.S. and Canadian governments. The court agreed and said the Ojibwes could hunt and fish on what had been their lands at the time these treaties were signed.

A press conference at the Mille Lacs Band reservation in Minnesota announcing the 1999 Supreme Court ruling upholding the treaty of 1837. This treaty allowed the Ojibwes to hunt and fish on land that had once belonged to them.

This angered many non-Natives, who now claimed ownership of the land and who fished the waters. They claimed that the Ojibwes were threatening the supply of fish, but this was proven in court to be incorrect. Instead, it was **pollutants** from non-Native industries and non-Native sports anglers who had reduced fish populations. The legal battles went all the way to the U.S. Supreme Court, which upheld the Ojibwes' rights to hunt and fish beyond the boundaries of the reservations. Today, white resort owners and sports anglers continue to harass Ojibwe fishermen despite court rulings.

Literature, Art, and Sports

Louise Erdrich has written children's books and novels such as *Tracks*. In many of them she writes about how the loss of land, children, and cultural traditions to whites' assimilation policies affect Ojibwe families. Her characters rely on humor and strong ties to traditions to get them through often harsh lives.

Comedian Rebecca Belmore uses humor and funny costumes in her performances to get non-Natives to see just how "really, really silly" movies are in the way they show Natives acting and talking. Her shows at the Canadian Museum of Civilization in Hull, Quebec, include "(I'm a) High-Tech Teepee Trauma Mama."

Ojibwe Comic Books

The Mille Lacs Band in Minnesota developed its first educational comic book in 1996 as an "opportunity to share our **heritage** and culture with others," explains Melanie Benjamin, chief executive of the Mille Lacs Band. Their second comic book was released in 1999.

In *A Hero's Voice*, Georgie and Jennie learn about true heroic Ojibwe (Anishinaabe) leaders by listening to their grandfather's stories. In *Dreams of Looking Up*, Mary and her family discover the importance of their people's traditions, customs, and culture.

A cultural tile mural created at the Mille Lacs Band's Nay Ah Shing school.

Artist Ron Noganosh also uses humor to get the meaning of his art across to people. "If they stop and laugh I got their attention, and then maybe they'll take the time to look around at it a little bit more and see what's going on," he explains. Many of his works were created from items people have thrown away. In his sculpture *Will the Turtle Be Unbroken?* Planet Earth, dying from pollution, sits on a turtle shell that is carried through space on the starship *Enterprise.*

Ojibwes have also made their mark in sports. In pro hockey 1997 National Hockey League (NHL) Coach of the Year Ted Nolan and Chris Simon of the 1996 Stanley Cup Champion Colorado Avalanche credit their achievements to the cultural traditions their parents taught them — traditions like working together, respecting elders, and making decisions as a group.

Chris Simon credits his success in hockey to the cultural traditions of his Ojibwe family.

Contemporary Life

Ojibwe families who live on reservations today remain very close. Parents, children, grandparents, and other relatives get together often. They continue the tradition of hospitality and concern for their relatives and community. Ojibwes on and off the reservation try to help each other and work for their communities to keep them strong.

On or off the reservation, Ojibwes live in the same types of houses as non-Natives. Ojibwes own TVs, radios, computers, video games, stoves, refrigerators, cars, and telephones. Like the rest of the world, bands are linked by high-speed Internet connections.

Children play ball in the yard, go to school, and do homework. Many speak three languages — English, French, and Ojibwe. Some take part in traditional ceremonies and have learned how to build birch-bark canoes, weave baskets, or bead clothing. They also help their relatives harvest wild rice and maple sugar.

Today, Ojibwe still harvest *manomin*, wild rice, in the traditional way. One person uses long poles to push the canoes through the fields, while another uses cedar sticks to bend the stalks and knock the grain into the canoe.

I may be an Urban Indian, but . . . the reserve is still deep within me. . . . As my mother says, I know home will always be there. So will the mosquitoes and the gossip and the relatives who still treat you like you are twelve years old . . . and those who walk in my moccasins know the rest.

Drew Hayden Taylor in Funny, You Don't look Like One: Observations from a Blue-Eyed Ojibway, *1998*

26

Slot machines at Mille Lacs Reservation Grand Casino in Minnesota. Money generated by casino gambling has enabled the Ojibwes to start their own schools where children can learn about traditional culture and language.

Tribal **casinos** on U.S. reservations have provided Ojibwes with jobs and money for other enterprises such as a horse-breeding business, craft shops, construction companies, and medical clinics. Ojibwes in the United States and Canada focus strongly on housing and educating their people. Tribal colleges in both countries celebrate cultural understanding by promoting the language, culture, and history of the Ojibwes.

Nay Ah Shing Schools

In 1999, the Mille Lacs Band opened the Nay Ah Shing primary and secondary schools. The schools are a major step forward in the Ojibwes' efforts to recover their cultural heritage. Twelve teachers instruct 270 students in the Ojibwe language. Students learn the language and history and participate in traditional activities such as gathering rice, making maple sugar, hunting, fishing, and drumming.

Here an Ojibwe student at a Nay Ah Shing school uses a computer to learn about his special cultural heritage.

Time Line

1622	First contact between Ojibwes (Anishinaabeg) and Europeans (French traders).
1659	Daniel du Luth negotiates a peace agreement between the Ojibwes and the Dakotas.
1727-45	War breaks out between the Ojibwes and Dakotas over French trade.
1745-50	Ojibwes settle in the region of Lake Mille Lacs in modern Minnesota.
1760	The British take control of Canada from the French.
1783	The Treaty of Paris splits the Ojibwes' territory between Canada and the U.S.
1825	Treaty council held at Prairie du Chien, Wisconsin, establishes the boundaries between the Ojibwes and Dakotas.
1837	The Treaty of 1837 protects hunting, fishing and gathering rights on Ojibwe lands taken by the U.S. government.
1850	Canadian government and Ojibwes sign Robinson Superior Treaty.
1855	The Mille Lacs Band sign a treaty that creates a 61,000-acre (24,700-ha) reservation at Lake Mille Lacs; the U.S. government also negotiates with other bands, promising to create reservations around eastern Michigan, which it never does.
1862	The Dakota War begins; Mille Lacs Band warriors end up defending non-Natives.
1880s	U.S. government passes assimilation policies.
1891	U.S. Congress declares all Native children must attend boarding schools.
1902	U.S. government officials sell land on the Mille Lacs Reservation and force members of that band to move to White Earth Reservation.
1934	Congress passes the Indian Reorganization Act, recognizing indigenous people's right to self-government.
1942	The Canadian government illegally seizes the majority of the Stony Point Reserve, forcibly relocating the Band to the nearby Kettle Point Reserve.
1968	Three Ojibwes found the American Indian Movement in Minneapolis, Minnesota.
1974-77	Ojibwes of Sabaskong Bay in Ontario defy the Canadian government and begin running their own schools.
1984-94	Five reservations are established in Michigan.
1999	U.S. Supreme Court upholds the Treaty of 1837, stating that Ojibwes have a treaty right to hunt, fish, and gather on lands taken away from them by the government; Ojibwes continue to be harassed when trying to hunt or fish as guaranteed by treaty.

Glossary

alliance: an agreement between two groups to work together on a common goal.

ancestor: a person from whom an individual or group is descended.

assimilate: to bring into conformity with the customs and attitudes of a group or nation.

broadcloth: a thick cloth woven from wool.

casinos: buildings that have slot machines, card games, and other gambling games.

clan: a group of related families.

consensus: an agreement among all individuals in a group to an opinion or position.

elder: an older person.

heritage: cultural traditions that are passed down from grandparents and parents to children for many years.

indigenous: originating in a particular country or region.

negotiate: to discuss with others to come to an agreement.

pollutants: substances that make air, water, or land dirty or impure.

prophesy: to tell of something that one feels will happen in the future.

quest: an adventurous journey to seek something.

tan: to make into leather by soaking an animal skin in a special solution.

treaties: agreements between several nations.

visions: things that are not from this world but the supernatural one; visions resemble dreams, but the person is awake.

wampum belts: different-colored beads made from shells strung into belts in unique designs, which serve as reminders of historical events, laws, and treaties.

More Resources

Web Sites:

http://www.sfo.com/~denglish/fishweirs Tells the history of Mnikaning — a traditional fish weir site in Canada — along with Ojibwe history.

http://www.tolatsga.org/ojib.html Explains words from the fur trade era in Ojibwe, French, and English.

http://www.kstrom.net/isk/food/wildrice.html Tells the story of Ojibwe wild rice gathering.

http://www.kstrom.net/isk/food/maple.html Tells the story of Ojibwe sugar bush camps.

Videos:

Enduring Ways of the Lac du Flambeau People. WDSE TV, [no date].

A Gift to One, A Gift to Many: James Jackson Sr., Ojibwe Medicine Man. WDSE TV, 1993.

Ikwe. National Film Board of Canada, [no date].

Rice Harvest. National Film Board of Canada, 1980.

The Woodlands: The Story of the Mille Lacs Ojibwe. Mille Lacs Band of Ojibwe Indians, [no date].

Books:

Goff, Cindy, and Steve Premo. *A Hero's Voice.* Mille Lacs Band of Ojibwe, 1996.

Goff, Cindy. *Dreams of Looking Up.* Mille Lacs Band of Ojibwe Indians, 1999.

Smith, Cynthia Leitch, and Cornelius Van Wright. *Jingle Dance.* Morrow Junior, 2000.

Smith, Cynthia Leitch. *Rain Is Not My Indian Name.* HarperCollins Juvenile Books, 2001.

Things to Think About and Do

A Variety of Homes

The Ojibwes' neighbors to the West were the Dakotas and to the East were the Haudenosaunees. Each of these Native peoples lived in very different types of houses. Research these houses on the web or in books. Draw a Dakota teepee, an Ojibwe wigwasigamig, and a Haudenosaunee longhouse. Write about how each of these homes is different from the others.

Country Life, City Life

Many Ojibwes were forced to move to cities during the 1950s. How would life be different for these people who had grown up gathering wild rice, making maple sugar, growing vegetables, hunting game, and fishing? Write an essay on what you think.

Ojibwe Beading

Look at the designs shown on the cover and on page 5 of this book. Using beads, paste, and a piece of cloth, create a floral design similar to the ones Ojibwes sewed on their clothing.

Creative Recycling

Ojibwe Artist Ron Noganosh uses odds and ends that people usually throw away to create his artwork. Collect some items from home and see what sort of artwork you can create.

Index